RELATIONSHIP
RESTORED

A GUIDE TO CROSS' BASEMENT THEORY
FOR COUPLES CONFLICT RESOLUTION

DOLPHY F. CROSS

HIGHERLIFE
PUBLISHING & MARKETING

Published by HigherLife Development Services Inc.
PO Box 623307
Oviedo, Florida 32762
www.ahigherlife.com

Paperback ISBN: 9798989529445
eBook ISBN: 9798989529483

Printed in the United States of America.

Dedication

This book is first dedicated to Beverly, my wife, my friend, my care partner, and my partner in ministry. Secondly, it is dedicated to all those in the pastoral counseling ministry and caring professions. Finally, it is dedicated to all couples struggling to keep their marriages and relationships together, and ultimately, to all our children.

Contents

Acknowledgments

I owe the completion of this work to my dear wife, Beverly, to whom I have dedicated this book. It all began with continued encouragement from my son Dolmar, who felt that the responses from churches inviting me to make family presentations were always so positive that I should publish my work and make it available to other pastors and practitioners.

I also want to thank Dr. Richard Behers, retired Director of Spiritual Care for the Cornerstone Hospice in Florida, CPE supervisor, and author. Although I had not known him for very long, his counsel and dedication to excellence and professionalism in chaplaincy made an indelible impression on me. I wish to thank all the couples who allowed me to use this tool in their counseling encounter and who, in turn, encouraged me to continue using it due to its effectiveness.

Finally, I wish to acknowledge all the pastors and pastoral counselors who have read the manuscript and encouraged me to make haste and get it published. This includes Chaplain Patrick Brown, who felt that the technique was so positive and effective that I should waste no time getting it copyrighted. I wish to also express my appreciation to him for editing this book in preparation for printing the second edition.

Introduction

While some societies remain focused on prevention and curative measures as it relates to health and well-being, most of North America has *evolved into symptom management.*

This is generally seen in the physical and mental healthcare industries. It has now made its way into the psychological and counseling fields. What we need is the ability to diagnose and treat the root cause so we can accomplish the task of restoring broken relationships.

Cross' Basement Theory for Couples Conflict Resolution (BTCCR) seeks to bridge the gap between symptom treatment and treating the root causes of couples in conflict. In the interest of clarity, the words *tool* and *technique* will be used interchangeably to identify the *Basement Theory*. The abbreviated acronym "BTCCR"

> **BTCCR seeks to bridge the gap between symptom treatment and treating the root causes of couples in conflict.**

will also be used to identify the *Basement Theory for Couples Conflict Resolution.*

Finally, the New King James Version (NKJV) is used throughout this book unless otherwise stated. Conflict in a relationship as intimate as marriage is unavoidable because marriage is never between identical twins. The differences in personalities and characters will invariably spawn conflict. This also means that anywhere two people are there is a potential for conflict. The emphatic and undisputable reality is that all couples have conflicts. Therefore, conflict should never become the issue and should never be the cause of separation and divorce for a Christian couple. Sadly, however, this is not the case even in the church. The divorce rate is on the increase even among Christian couples. There is a definitive need for a tool such as ***Cross' Basement Theory for Couples Conflict Resolution*** (BTCCR).

This book introduces the specific technique for all pastors and professional counselors to utilize and unlock doors through which answers may be found. Answers that can potentially bring to a screeching halt or at least minimize the dysfunction of lingering and prolonged conflicts between couples. God desires to see those who believe in Him coexist in love, whether married or unmarried (1 John 4:7). The richness and practical nature of this technique and its simplicity for understanding and interpretation are added advantages to pastors who are not clinically trained. It is a proven technique that has been met with resounding success since its introduction well over twelve years ago.

Restoring broken relationships is one of the reasons for Christ's coming to this earth. The human family is not just fractured but broken. Therefore, Jesus gave His church the ministry of reconciliation so that we can have broken relationships restored (2 Cor. 5:18–19).

Three vignettes will be shared using pseudo-names to protect the privacy of the individuals. The section on homework is there to help couples understand that they will have to do their part in eradicating repeating conflicts in their marriage.

May this book prove to be a blessing to all pastors and chaplains in their respective marriages, and may they become living examples to their congregations and those under their care as they seek to restore broken relationships.

Conflict Resolution

Conflicts occur when two or more people or groups attempt to occupy the same space at the same time. Not all conflicts can be resolved—some will have to be managed. A conflict can be healthy and can create a fertile environment for growth between the couple. According to Larry Crabb (1977), effective counseling is centrally and critically a relationship between people who care. Worthington (1999) recognized conflicting couples as those who regularly fight over issues without arriving at a mutually acceptable resolution.

Wise counsel may be just what the doctor ordered to reconcile differences (Prov. 19:20). Christian couples are not immune to conflict. If they are not taught how to handle it when it shows up, their marriage can become another statistic.

Effective counseling is built on a relationship of trust between the client and the counselor. Counseling is not a discipline like dentistry or medicine, which depends fundamentally upon a growing amount of technical knowledge administered by highly trained professionals. Professional and pastoral counselors alike tend to rely on a few techniques with two or three basic principles, perhaps without ever clearly thinking through exactly why their counseling efforts should work (Crabb 1977). *Cross' Basement Theory for Couples Conflict Resolution* (BTCCR) is a technique that can be used as a diagnostic tool for couples in conflict.

Ronald Richardson's book about couples in conflict emphasizes *Family Systems Theory* and how it impacts conflict, the counseling processes, and phases. The book challenges the counselor to adopt a theory and strive to perfect its use in his or her counseling practice (Richardson 2010). Interestingly, Richardson did not use the word *theory* to mean a hunch. He alluded to Dr. Murray Bowen, who used the term as a scientist would—a formal statement about how things work (Richardson 2010). Learning about *Bowen's Family Systems Theory* and understanding the family as an emotional unit is advisable. With the understanding of the family as an emotional unit, the perceived individual issue(s)

With the understanding of the family as an emotional unit, the perceived individual issue(s) is not viewed as limited to the individual but in the context of the family unit.

is not viewed as limited to the individual but in the context of the family unit.

Life is all about relationships, and in general, there are only two types of relationships. The vertical relationship between mankind and God and the horizontal relationship between mankind and his fellowman (Eph. 4:32). *Hope-Focused Marriage Counseling* (Worthington 2013) and *Couples in Conflict* (Richardson 2010) are the recommended books to be used with **Cross' Basement Theory.** Like other forms of counseling, these books are focused on improving relationships, and Worthington's book provides the perfect guide to *Brief Therapy.*

The main thesis of his book is the strengthening of marriages and reducing the incidences of divorce through spiritual interventions and the motivation of couples to strengthen their resolve while waiting on God's work in their marriage (Worthington 2013). Divorce was never in God's plan for man. Divorce is a result of sin and the hardness of man's heart (Matt. 19:3–12; Mark 10:2–12).

What Is the Cross Basement Theory?

Cross Basement Theory (BTCCR) is a diagnostic tool ideally suited for pre-marital and marital counseling to unmask potential problem areas for pre-marital couples and diagnose the primary cause of conflict between married couples. Interestingly, doctors would not prescribe or administer treatment without first checking the patient and doing a thorough assessment. Through tests and assessments, a proper diagnosis is made. Sometimes, the nature of the test result or diagnosis may necessitate consultation with a specialist.

The society in which we live today has evolved into a symptom management society. This is generally seen in the physical and mental healthcare industries. It has now made its way into the psychological and counseling fields. Many types of sicknesses are unduly prolonged, while others end in death due to the treatment of symptoms rather than addressing the root causes. While conflict in a relationship as delicate as marriage is expected, there is always a root cause to every conflict. A marriage stands a better chance of surviving if the couple knows the cause of their constant quarreling and fighting.

What we need is the ability to diagnose and treat root causes.

A proper diagnosis must be made before corrective treatment can be administered in the medical profession. Similarly, counselors should not begin counseling based only on the intake information or on the counselee's declaration of why they are seeking counsel. Typically, an assessment does not reveal the root cause of a conflict. Sometimes it takes several sessions before the hurting parties reach a level of transparency where they can eventually reveal their inner pain. BTCCR is a combination of diagnostic and *Theory-Based Assessments*. The following quote provides some context:

> **BTCCR is a diagnostic tool that can identify the real source of a couple's problems or areas of conflict.**

> A diagnostic assessment focuses on the client and the current and developmental context influencing the client. The diagnostic assessment focuses on gathering information about the client that is clinically relevant to

the treatment process and outcomes. (Sperry 2012, 163)

This diagnostic assessment seeks to minimize the counseling time by answering the question of what brings about the couple's conflict and diminishing relationship for which they now seek counsel or therapy. It allows the counselor to get to the root cause of the conflict. The diagnostic assessment, however, will not indicate how the conflict began or how to resolve it. This is the responsibility of the trained counselor or therapist. It is also advisable that the counselor gets acquainted with the *Theory-Based Assessment* approach. The *Theory-Based Assessment* works well with *Cognitive Behavioral Therapy*, and it is a valuable component of a comprehensive assessment strategy (Sperry 2012). A couple arguing over the flavor of the ice cream that was purchased may have nothing to do with the ice cream. *Cognitive Behavioral Therapy* would be an appropriate therapy intervention in such a case.

When an individual in excruciating abdominal pain visits the doctor, many times the patient's complaint has little if anything to do with the sickness he or she is experiencing. Unfortunately, many patients die because of an incorrect diagnosis and the wrong treatment being administered. Many stories are told of patients who died shortly after visiting their primary care physicians. Lives are saved after thorough patient assessments using interviews, tests, and diagnostic instruments to arrive at the correct diagnoses.

Cross' Basement Theory for Couples Conflict Resolution (BTCCR) is a diagnostic tool that can identify the real source of a couple's problems or areas of conflict. Correctly administered, honestly executed, and rightly interpreted, it can reveal the couple's potential areas of current or future conflict. This tool can pinpoint or diagnose areas of conflict among couples who have been married for one to ninety-nine years. BTCCR works well in pre-marital counseling to help couples discover the area or areas in their relationship that have the potential for conflict.

When a proper diagnosis is made, the counselor or therapist is then able to choose and apply appropriate counseling interventions that will address the couple's specific needs. This is the essence of *Brief Therapy* and solution-focused marriage counseling that the **Basement Theory** embraces. In this instance, the adages apply: *To be forewarned is to be forearmed*"; or "*An ounce of prevention is better than a pound of cure.*" A correct diagnosis also limits the number of counseling sessions needed to get the couple back on track. Therefore, *Solution-Focused Brief Therapy* is the main model chosen for counseling interventions with **Cross' Basement Theory**. It focuses on solutions that result in healing for the couple in counseling.

The foundation for the **Basement Theory** is love and hope. Love is a central value in every marriage or relationship built on hopeful aspirations. For a troubled marriage to be fixed, hope must become a realistic factor for both parties. Marriage counseling deals with people's culture, beliefs, social orientation, and values within the context of solving marital problems so that the couple will be more loving. "Hope-focused marriage counseling is focused on building hope. Working on the marriage requires hope. Hope provides the motivation to work" (Worthington 1999, 30). Love cannot thrive in an atmosphere of bitterness, resentment, and disrespect. Hope, belief, and values are all part of the solution process.

Does the Basement Theory Work in Any Culture?

Conflicts are not gender- or culture-specific. Anywhere two people are, there is the potential for conflict. Therefore, BTCCR is a conflict resolution tool that is designed for use in any culture and with any couple regardless of age. Despite the proven effectiveness of this tool, success is dependent on the honesty of the participants and their willingness to execute the requirements of BTCCR. While this tool can be used effectively in any language or culture—and by anyone—it was specifically designed to be faith-based within the context of Christian counseling.

God created human beings in His image and man was to have dominion over all of God's creation (Gen. 1:26–27). The reflection of God's image continues in all people regardless of age, sex, skin color, or moral condition. A newborn baby does not become a human by displaying qualities of the environment in his or her behavior and responses. The baby is a human even before birth. *"Behold, children are a heritage of the Lord; the fruit of the womb is a reward*" (Psa. 127:3). This reality leads us to understand that because of the Adamic sin, each child is born with the natural propensities and proclivities to sin. Sin, therefore, is an inescapable reality due to the original sin.

The sin problem cannot be corrected without the Word of God and divine intervention. Sin deforms humanity in more ways than just the physical. Therefore, there is a need for spiritual, physical, and psychological healing. Scripture teaches that mankind was born in sin and shaped in iniquity (Psa. 51:5). All of humanity is, therefore, deformed and needs to be made whole. "The literal meaning of healing is becoming whole" (Walsh 2009, 35). Healing is a process that we are always involved in. There is and will always be something to improve on, something that we could do better. Healing is a fact of life and a reality that we must all accept before any real change can come.

Different types of sicknesses will necessitate different forms of healing. Some people are sick physically, emotionally, mentally, or spiritually. Interestingly, some people experience all the different types of sicknesses at the same time. "Sometimes people heal physically but not heal emotionally, mentally, or spiritually; badly strained relationships may remain unhealed" (Walsh 2009, 35). Whether physical, emotional, mental, or spiritual, all true healing comes from God, as demonstrated by Jesus Christ when He walked this earth (Mark 5:25–34; Luke 7:2–10; John 9:1–11). The Christian counselor knows that there is a biblical solution to every problem. He or she knows also that Jesus was tested *"in all points ... as we are"* (Heb. 4:15), and He successfully met every temptation without sinning (Heb. 4:14–16; Matt. 4:1–10). There is no cultural barrier to God's power to set men and women free from sin. It is the task of the Christian counselor to understand your problem, help you discover God's solution to it,

> **There is no cultural barrier to God's power to set men and women free from sin. It is the task of the Christian counselor to understand your problem, help you discover God's solution to it, and to encourage you to do what God requires you to do about it.**

and encourage you to do what God requires you to do about it (Adams 1973). This establishes that every pastor needs to take time to understand how to administer this diagnostic tool called **Cross' Basement Theory for Couples Conflict Resolution** (BTCCR).

The Christian counselor does not embrace the theories of men for solutions to spiritual issues as manifested in the problems of life. Without a clear understanding of how problems develop, counseling can become nothing more than a warm, friendly conversation full of good intentions (Crabb 1997). The counselor must create a healing environment by laying the proper foundation for honest communication to remove the pain caused by sin. According to Walsh (2009), the ultimate desired outcome is to create a healing environment for family members that relieves their suffering from experiences of illness.

If there is anything that must be maintained at all costs, it is the integrity of the Scriptures as the authoritative standard for Christian counseling (Adams 1973). The Christian counselor must keep in mind that the basic need of people is to be born again or regenerated. Once that has become their experience, they need to be instructed towards Christ-centeredness in all their living (Kent Sr. 1974). This can only be accomplished by a man or woman of faith who has also experienced hope. This also helps to establish the relevance and the need for Christian counseling today.

Every counselee needs hope and meaning regardless of their culture, creed, or nation. Without hope, the Christian counselor cannot communicate the hope and encouragement that many counselees need (Adams 1973, 48). God instilled hope in Adam just after the fall (Gen. 3:15), because like Adam, sin has worked its defeating and disheartening effects in all our lives. There are times when every Christian is dispirited. Hope and love must be the unwritten recurring theme in every counseling session. Hope helps to give zest to life and allows one to face each day with optimistic expectancy.

Therapy Interventions That Complement the Basement Theory Technique

Many different therapies and counseling interventions are used to impact counseling today. However, the therapies that work best with BTCCR are *Solution-Focused Brief Therapy, Cognitive Behavioral Therapy,* and *Couples Therapy.* Each of these therapies will be briefly highlighted. The Christian counselor and therapist must understand that there is no "one size fits all" in counseling; therefore, other theories of interventions can be explored.

Solution-Focused Brief Therapy (SFBT) is concerned with an individual's present and future as well as the individual's goals. It is a goal-oriented therapy that places little or no emphasis on past experiences or circumstances. Therefore, the issues that brought a couple to counseling are generally not the issues targeted by the counselor. The issue that brought the patient to the doctor may not be the root cause of the illness. SFBT is not confined to *Couples Therapy;* it also works well with individual and family therapies.

Cognitive Behavioral Therapy (CBT) is a psycho-social intervention that is the most widely used evidence-based practice for improving mental health. Guided by empirical research, CBT focuses on the development of personal coping strategies that target solving current problems and changing unhelpful patterns. Like SFBT, CBT is also a goal-oriented psychotherapy that takes a practical approach to problem-solving and conflict resolution. It is also short term in its interventions and scope.

Caring and nurturing couples (and the congregation as a whole) cannot be approached like an annual physical examination. *Couples Therapy* must be integrated into a pastor's preaching and teaching from the pulpit.

Couples Therapy (CT) is a branch of general *Family Therapy. Couples Therapy* can be a significant help to couples experiencing difficulty in their marriage. *Couples Therapy* is also a good intervention in pre-marital counseling and, therefore, works well in the **Basement Theory**. *Couples Therapy* is a needed intervention for couples in counseling and should be considered a safe choice in general couples counseling. Christians. like everyone, are sometimes confronted with serious marital issues. Caring and nurturing couples (and the congregation as a whole) cannot be approached like an annual physical examination. *Couples Therapy* must be integrated into a pastor's preaching and teaching from the pulpit.

The Technique and Its Interpretation

Setting up the appointment is very important to the successful completion of the process. Whether the counselor or the intake secretary takes the call, it is important to adhere to the following on the telephone: (1) stick to the intake questionnaire once the caller establishes the reason for the call; (2) share with the prospective counselee the available counseling slots and confirm a date; (3) discuss cost payment options and method of payment; and (4) stress the importance of being on time. Richardson (2010) suggests that "the counselor should never allow the first contact with the counselee over the phone to become a counseling session. They will, quite automatically, tell us about the problem from their point of view. They may have already diagnosed the problem, who is at fault, and suggest what we should do to help" (99). The counseling session should begin in the office.

The counselor or assistant should welcome the couple. Assessment is an ongoing process that begins from the moment of entering the office. They would be led to the counseling room or office, where they would be given instructions relative to using the tool. The instructions include: (1) a commitment to honesty; (2) no communication between them while fulfilling the requirements of the BTCCR; and (3) following the instructional guidelines. After about ten to fifteen minutes, the counselor enters the room, collects the completed information, and explains how the interpretation will be done. If the process seems intimidating, I can assure you it is not. It is probably easier than applying for a credit card. The main requirement is the need for honesty.

To begin the interpretation, and in the interest of full disclosure, it is recommended that the counselor or pastor informs the couple that he or she is a Christian counselor who relies on Scripture as the foundation for counseling before opening the session with prayer. This prayer is especially important and should include God as the creator of the marriage institution and Satan as the destroyer of everything good. The couple's names should also be mentioned in the prayer, including an invitation for the Holy Spirit to take control and direct the session. This prayer should set the atmosphere for a spiritual encounter and re-establish that the couple is in the presence of the Holy Spirit to be guided by a Christian counselor.

Jay Adams asserts, "If there is anything that must be maintained at all costs, it is the integrity of the Scriptures as the authoritative standard for Christian counseling" (1973, 18). Adams further asserts, "It is only upon biblical presuppositions that counseling can be based, and these are necessarily the same for every Christian counselor" (1973, 18). The couple needs to perceive the counselor as being spiritually connected to begin the counseling relationship.

At this point, each party is handed a pre-marked Bible at 1 Corinthians 13. It is important to pre-mark this chapter rather than assume that the couple can find it independently. The couple is then asked to read alternate verses slowly, but both are to read the last verse together. This is followed by a brief over-view of *Solution-Focused Brief Therapy* as the counseling model and intervention of choice.

Notice that up to this point, the couple that comes for counseling has not been asked any specific question(s) concerning their marriage. By this time, the couple should be more relaxed, more informed about the counseling process, and more trusting of the counselor. It is important to build a relationship of trust between the counselees and the counselor. Those few moments help to build that relationship, so the couple is more at ease and less on guard.

The counselor then turns to each and asks, "Why are you here, and what are your expectations from this session?" The reason for this compound question is to sensitize the couple to the reality that every counseling session should have a goal and an expected outcome. This question helps the couple to set the goal or goals and lay the foundation to begin their solution-focused encounter. It is the responsibility of the counselor to keep in front of the couple their goal and expected outcome as the session progresses. It is easy to lose sight of the goal in counseling because of heightened tension and expressed frustration between the couple. The set goals should be practical and achievable. Additionally, every effort should be made by the counselor to guide the couple in achieving those goals.

> The *Basement Theory* helps a couple to know what each other is thinking because it is expressed as part of the BTCCR priority listing.

Ordering your priority is the foundation on which the *Basement Theory* is built. People are different and consequently will also have different priorities in life. Selfishness and lack of spiritual guidance can cause one to have misplaced priorities. It only takes one misplaced priority to create a serious conflict in a marriage. It is important, therefore, to have one's priorities straight. A strong marriage is rooted in Christian love, honest communication, mutual respect, and a commitment to trust each other.

People are in a constant process of change. The couple that goes to bed after deciding on a particular subject matter will sometimes wake up the following morning with different viewpoints. The *Basement Theory* can be used to assess your marriage as it relates to changing values and priorities. In essence, your values will determine your priorities, and your values are revealed in your behavior and lifestyle. Pastors and their spouses are particularly encouraged to apply the *Basement Theory* exercise at least once every two years because we are prone to being influenced by a culture of changing values. Speaking from personal experience, this has been a blessing in my marriage as my spouse and I put this counsel into practice. A pastor's marriage, like any other marriage, can stretch like cheap fabric. If left unchecked, it can result in separation or divorce—leaving the children as collateral damage and victims.

On the eve of sending this manuscript to the publisher in September 2018, the news came out that a pastor just committed suicide in California. While the details of that sad occurrence were not available, the sad reality is that a wife had become a widow, and three children were left fatherless. What could have driven a pastor to commit suicide? The truth may never be revealed—it is interred with his bones. This lingering question searches for an answer, however. Could this have been avoided? I invite you, the reader, to arrive at your conclusion. No man is an island; no man stands alone, and everybody needs somebody sometimes. Everyone needs a friend or two in this life. The first and most important friend to have is Jesus, the friend with whom you speak every day but cannot see with your physical eyes. The second friend should be your spouse, the one with whom you communicate and share every day—the one whom you can touch and feel.

A relationship as intimate as marriage thrives on daily communication to establish and maintain harmony. Similar goals and aspirations breathe harmony and happiness. Mahatma Gandhi once said, *"Happiness is when what you think, what you say, and what you do are in harmony."* Happiness, according to the songwriter, is to know the Savior, and to live a life in His favor. The **Basement Theory** helps a couple to know what each other is thinking because it is expressed as part of the BTCCR priority listing. This generally creates talking points for the couple. Love and honesty are the keys to an accurate diagnosis and corresponding interpretation.

While the **Basement Theory's** primary goal is to diagnose the cause of conflict(s) in a marriage, it also can help couples adjust in response to misplaced priorities. A couple can have similar values and priorities, but those priorities can be misplaced over time and create the same conflict as though the priorities did not exist. That is why couples with similar religious and social backgrounds tend to be more successful in their marriage relationships.

Stephen Grunlan (1984) states, "Values are the criteria we use to define what is good or bad, beautiful, or ugly, moral or immoral, worthwhile or not worthwhile. Our values are important to us and form the basis for most of our decisions" (80-81). He expounds further by making the case for religion and finances as values that relate to primary areas of life (Grunlan 1984). Every couple deserves the opportunity to know what those differences are, and their potential to trigger conflicts in a marriage.

Ordering Your Priority

Please list the following on the left in order of **your** priority on the right.

Name:_____

Age:_____

Marital Status: _____

Telephone #: _____

1. Religion/Church	1.	_____
2. Love	2.	_____
3. God	3.	_____
4. House	4.	_____
5. Marriage	5.	_____
6. Children	6.	_____
7. Education/School	7.	_____
8. Sex	8.	_____
9. Communication	9.	_____
10. Family Time	10.	_____
11. Money/Savings	11.	_____
12. Car	12.	_____
13. In-Laws	13.	_____
14. Friends	14.	_____
15. Work/Job	15.	_____
16. Freedom/Independence	16.	_____

The **Basement Theory** was designed for couples counseling in general but specifically for Christian counselors. It must be emphasized that there is a difference between pastoral counseling as a profession and pastors who do counseling. Christian counseling, in essence, is clothed in the person of Christ (Col. 1:26–27). Christ is the ultimate caregiver, and the apostle Paul counsels us to follow his example as he follows the example of Christ (1 Cor. 11:1). Christ Himself is challenging the church, and the application of Christian counseling in all its varieties is one answer to that challenge (Clinton et al. 2005, 29). The ultimate purpose is that of restoring relationships with God and with each other.

BTCCR is a tremendous breakthrough for pastors and Christian counselors who normally must spend hours in different counseling sessions before getting to the root of the problem.

The **Basement Theory** is a straightforward diagnostic tool that all pastors of any religion can utilize. It is used specifically to diagnose the cause of conflict between married couples and pinpoint potential conflict areas in pre-marital counseling. According to Sperry (2012), "A diagnostic assessment is a focused assessment of the client and the current and developmental context influencing the client" (163). The **Basement Theory** reveals the root cause of a couple's conflict, opens a window into the way the couple socializes, and reveals what influences their decision-making and priorities.

It is the responsibility of the pastor to seek professional training and provide the needed counseling to meet the diagnostic results of the technique. According to Richardson (2010), ongoing supervision is essential to being a consistently good counselor. Simply being a good pastor or a caring person is not enough. Today's pulpits need pastors who are sensitive to the mental, physical, social, and marital struggles that a congregation undergoes. Counseling cannot be confined to the office. The church at worship on any given day can be transformed into a large therapy class. The pastor can address any of the identified subjects on mental health, physical health, or marital well-being.

Unfortunately, no one pastor is equipped with all the skillsets to satisfy the needs and demands of a diverse congregation. The other unfortunate reality is that some pastors do not seem to realize their limitations and consequently refuse to seek outside help. This leadership approach stunts the growth of any congregation—and anything that is not growing is dying. Like any living organism, a body of believers can only grow in the right environment. That environment is largely determined by the pastor, the shepherd of the flock, who is charged with the responsibility to lead them to greener pastures and clean refreshing waters. The body of Christ, which is the church, thrives best in an atmosphere of interdependency (Matt. 18:15–20; Rom. 12:3–8; 1 Cor. 12:13).

Pastors must know their limitations when it comes to pastoral counseling. It is irresponsible and unethical not to have training and supervision in place if pastors want to provide regular counseling to their parishioners (Richardson 2010). ***Cross' Basement Theory for Couples Conflict Resolution*** (BTCCR) is a tremendous breakthrough for pastors and Christian counselors who normally must spend hours in different counseling sessions before getting to the root of the problem. Our prayer is for this tool to be made available to all pastors and for them to grasp the concept so that they can effectively employ it in their counseling ministries to their parishioners.

Counseling can be more effective when it is approached from a coaching standpoint. Counseling, on the one hand, can become superficial and mechanical, with a punctiliar effect after the counselees leave the office. Coaching, on the other hand, is more personal and has a linear effect that continues after the counselees leave the office and is conducive to faster healing. After the coaching is over, the burden is on the counselees to continue practicing the technique on their own. According to Richardson (2010), "Coaching takes the focus off the counselor/counselee relationship. It makes it clear that 'the game' is out there, elsewhere in the counselee's life" (95). This is one of the reasons why homework is mandatory and is important in the counseling process. It guarantees that the counselees continue to work on themselves while at home.

The presence of a neutral third-party counselor/coach is needed to help bridge the gap in an emotionally-charged relationship to provide guidance and place the burden of responsibility on themselves for their response (Richardson 2010).

A good counselor/coach will provide the counselee with the necessary tools to work with while at home. For the members of the clergy reading this, look introspectively now and waste not another day. Take your spouse by the hand and be vulnerable and transparent—confess and seek forgiveness; then you both can reach out for help together. You can trust God to keep His promise to you. He promised never to leave you (Heb. 13:15; Matt. 28:24).

8

Setting the Counseling Agenda

The counselor looks at the completed BTCCR by the couples and compares the priorities to determine existing or potential conflict. If the male lists God as his number one priority and the female lists God as her number one priority, there is no potential conflict with their belief or acceptance of God as being sovereign. However, if the male places God at number one and the female puts God at number four, this would be considered a red flag and, consequently, a possible area of present or future conflict. If the female places God at number three instead of four, this would be considered the safe zone with the least possibility for conflict.

If the female places love at number five and the male puts love at number two, this is a red flag. The counselor should then find out what the male has at his number five and where the female places that same topic. This technique results in the couple setting a personalized counseling agenda according to the number of red flags raised. A proper interpretation is necessary to arrive at a correct diagnosis.

It must be noted that each red flag is a subject for counsel because it reveals a present or future conflict. While it is prudent and necessary to provide general counsel, the BTCCR reveals areas in the couple's lives where conflicts exist or could exist in the future. The solution-focused counselor or therapist must now give priority to these revealed areas of conflict or potential conflict. This is the time to ask searching questions of the couple and activate the *Basement Theory*. This gives the advantage of providing specific counsel and makes the entire counseling experience solution-focused.

No red flags may show up. In such a case, the counselor should highly commend the couple and explain the reason why there are none and what that means. The counselor, at this juncture, would listen to the stories of the counselee to understand their premise and issue(s). No red flag means no "basement" issue. It is also possible to have no red flags if the couple is not being honest in completing the instrument.

If one of the red flags concerns finances, the counselor is responsible for asking specific questions to uncover the identified problem area. The counselor would then select the appropriate questions for a pre-marital or married couple in conflict. Such questions may include but are not limited to the following, which were adapted from Clinton, Hart, and Ohlschlager (2005), and Clinton and Trent (2009):

1. What is your current financial situation?
2. Do you have a student loan, and if yes, how much do you owe?
3. Have you both discussed this along with other debts you are carrying into the marriage?
4. What do you consider to be the cause of your financial concern or crisis today? Do you both agree that this is the source of the problem?
5. What do you think needs to happen for the concern to go away or to get out of this crisis?
6. How is this financial concern or crisis affecting your marriage and family?
7. How are you both currently coping with the situation?
8. Who usually handles the bills in your home? Describe the process for handling your monthly financial commitments.
9. What is the shortfall in what you need to meet those commitments? In what area can you peel back and save some money? Do you both think you can commit to tightening your belts for a while?

10. What lifestyle changes do you need to make to keep a financial crisis such as this from happening again?
11. Have you committed this situation to prayer?
12. Do you trust God to see you through this crisis?
13. Are you both willing to start praying together about this issue?
14. Are you willing to start praying right now, right here?

9

Pre-Marital Counseling

Pre-marital counseling is generally sought after and is a recommended intervention for those contemplating marriage. When a couple does not seek wise counsel, things can get messy very quickly. Consider the couple in the picture above. On the soles of the groom's shoes are the words, "*Help Me*," while on the soles of the bride's shoes are the words, "*Too Late*." Christian counselors should never join two people together in marriage without engaging them in pre-marital counseling. Marriage is a gift from God, and 1 Corinthians 13 is God's instruction to every couple. It would be in the best interest of every couple to memorize this chapter and put God's counsel into practice because a successful marriage does not just happen. Couples may be encouraged to read this chapter from a different translation than the King James Version. God wants you to have a successful marriage. While the meaning of the word *success* may differ for each individual or couple, a successful marriage involves a husband and wife working harmoniously together towards a common goal.

A healthy marriage calls for pre-marital preparation because most couples spend more time planning and preparing for the wedding as opposed to getting to know more about each other. Some potential married couples make the mistake of thinking that cohabitation will reveal their compatibility or incompatibility. As a result, they resort to "shacking up" and pretending to be married. This does not just affect their prospect for marriage, but it has a lasting moral, social, and spiritual impact—not just on their lives, but also on any children that result from such cohabitation.

Every prospective couple should be told that the marriage begins after the wedding. The preparation for a successful marriage begins with honest communication between the parties according to the principles recorded in Ephesians 4:25-32. If more couples were encouraged to work on communication issues at the start of their marriages, the need for future intervention would be minimal (Adams 1973). Remember—conflict is inevitable. How it is resolved or managed will determine marital success or failure.

Pre-marital counseling is geared to help the prospective couple successfully navigate the many twists and turns that will come up in a marriage. Cohabitation considerably lessens the chances of a successful marriage. Most people do not seek counsel before cohabitation; consequently, they are frequently unprepared to face or resolve this inevitable intruder called *conflict*. Honest and respectful communication that holds the key to marital bliss can end in a cul-de-sac because the cohabiting couple did not take the time to receive counsel against these pitfalls. The general assumption, however, is that Christians would take the principled and spiritually mature approach by rejecting cohabitation and embracing pre-marital counseling.

Pre-marital counseling for a Christian couple should not end without sessions on love, faith, hope, and forgiveness. Worthington (1999) suggests the counselor should promote love, faith, and work to help the couple or individual resolve relational issues. Sin is real and is the only cause of problems in the world. However, sin does not occur in a vacuum, but expresses itself through socialization, culture, values, and priorities. Christian married couples must understand these realities and they are best relayed through wisely structured pre-marital counseling utilizing the **Basement Theory** or other effective therapy.

The fact that a couple is in love and is excited about the prospects of becoming husband and wife does not shield them from the sin of fornication and other human errors. There are always habits, attitudes, and cultural proclivities to contend with that can trigger serious conflicts in a marriage. The **Basement Theory** is geared toward uncovering such issues that may not surface during courtship. The counseling provided should now be geared towards teaching the couple how to deal with those camouflaged challenges when they develop. The counseling should also be geared towards explaining how such conflicts can be identified, resolved, or avoided. Living models can be used to demonstrate successful marriages with the understanding that success does not mean perfection.

The Christian church and Christian marriages are in a dilemma partially due to a scarcity of role models. The church needs to give a platform and a voice to those whose marriages have aged well while experiencing scorching summers and shivering winters. These couples can share the love, commitment, and discipline that kept them together. According to Adams (1973), modeling is an essential biblical method for teaching. Modeling should not be confined to marriage but to every aspect of Christian living (2 Thess. 3:6–15). The apostle Paul was single, but he taught the relationship concepts that Christians should model (Phil. 4:9). Such a model not only brings honor to God but yields exponential rewards in our earthly existence. Examples are always more powerful than precepts, and a sermon lived is more effective than a sermon preached.

The Bible is still the fundamental guide for Christians contemplating marriage. Scripture provides one basic guiding principle—a prohibition against sexual intercourse before marriage (1 Cor. 6:9–20, 7:1–9; Gal. 5:19–21; Eph. 5:3). To succeed in this respect, Christian couples contemplating marriage must seek counsel to protect themselves against social and emotional issues that the Scripture does not address. Touching and kissing can lead to sexual stimulation, which involves caressing the genitals and fondling the breasts (Grunlan 1984). Young couples need to be aware of these potential pitfalls that can affect their marital relationship.

10

Post-Marital Counseling

Post-marital counseling is an idea that God has blessed me to develop, and this book is the medium chosen to introduce it in the Christian counseling arena. The idea of post-marital counseling was in response to many separations and divorces of young married couples in the recent decade. A companion book will be released in the fall of 2024 on the effects of prayer on marital stability. The essence of post-marital counseling is for couples who complete their pre-marital counseling to be asked to commit to returning six months after their wedding for post-marital counseling.

When a new vehicle is purchased, the dealership recommends servicing it after a certain number of miles or a specific period has elapsed. Similarly, the newly married couple may develop early conflicts in their marriage, and because of pride or fear of gossip, they refuse to seek early counseling intervention. These conflicts tend to escalate and deteriorate over time.

The post-marital counseling commitment helps to alleviate any feelings of pride that an early return for counseling might create. It contributes to removing the fear of anticipated gossip, which generally starts like this—they just got married and need counseling already! The couple's return for counseling should be based on a prior signed contract and memorandum of understanding. We have had several experiences where couples called in to arrange for an earlier post-marital visit before the agreed six months had elapsed. One couple erupted into a huge conflict while they were on their honeymoon. The post-marital counseling session provides the perfect opportunity for the counselor to determine root causes and apply appropriate interventions. Such guidance and support should keep the couple on track or get them back on track if they go off course.

Sometimes, individuals can mask or camouflage a behavior or character defect so well that it becomes undetectable during pre-marital counseling—especially during the first few sessions if this couple did not receive an intervention using the *Basement Theory*. This counseling intervention is likely most effective at unmasking this issue if honesty is present in the responses from the couple. The questions asked by the counselor would be based upon the diagnosed issue(s) resulting from applying the **Basement Theory**. The following counseling intervention is based on the concept of post-marital counseling with the pastoral counselor who conducted the pre-marital counseling with the couple.

Based on the pre-marital counseling the couple received, the counselor would begin the post-marital session as follows:

1. Ask, "How was the drive coming over?" Get the couple to respond to something that they need not think deeply about. Read their body language and facial expressions. Even the way they sit can tell a story, so be very observant of the couple and any cues presented—obvious or subtle. The purpose of the question that does not require deep introspection is to encourage a relaxed atmosphere. The couple could be experiencing serious issues and may even have argued last night or while on their way to the counseling office. The counselor should take nothing for granted.

2. Thank them for coming and open the session with prayer. The prayer should be specific to their visit and mention God who has the answer to every question and the solution to every problem. It is strongly recommended that they be given another diagnostic exercise using the **Cross' Basement Theory for Couples Conflict**

Resolution (BTCCR). This second exercise should be compared to the first to be used only as a reference by the counselor. Considering people are in a constant process of change, it should not be surprising to see that their priorities have changed.

3. Review expectations, whereby each one should show respect by listening without interrupting the other. It is important to lay down some ground rules for how you (the counselor) plan to proceed with the session. The question should then be asked: "So, who will go first in sharing your six months' progress and growth?" This is a time when the counselor takes notes while maintaining eye contact with both parties as much as possible. The tone of voice, posture, and general body language are important to observe at this point also. Expect the best after six months but never take it for granted that all is well. After listening to the other party, the counselor may seek to congratulate them on the marital progress and growth they have made as a couple or change course to address the issues or concerns they have raised. At this time, the counselor can share the comparative results of the second diagnostic exercise.

4. Depending on the outcome of their respective sharing, the counselor should have the following practical and spiritual questions ready:

   a. How are you both doing spiritually?

   b. How do you feel about your relationship with God at this point?

   c. Do you plan to make any lifestyle changes?

   d. What is your current financial situation?

   e. Are you practicing Christian benevolence and are you tithing?

   f. Who was chosen to handle the bills?

   g. What are your short-term and long-term goals?

   h. Are you praying together, and have you seen an answer to any of your prayers?

   i. What new insights have you gained about each other?

   j. If you could make one request of your spouse, what would that be?

5. There should be no scheduled return visit after a post-marital session. However, if a couple un-covers an issue(s) that must be addressed before the counselor, additional session(s) should be arranged before they leave the office. A regular post-marital session should not go beyond two hours. The *Solution-Focused Brief Therapy* mod-el that the **Basement Theory** embraces does not

commit counselees to six, eight, or ten sessions to achieve the counseling goals and objectives.

6. As mentioned before, post-marital counseling sessions share some similarities with the tune-up for a new vehicle purchase. Just as it is necessary to have regularly scheduled tune-ups for optimal service and performance from the vehicle, it is also important to have scheduled visits to your family counselor to maintain a quality relationship and a healthy, balanced marriage.

7. In the modern world, responsible people who care about their health go to see their doctor for annual physicals. They have annual and sometimes twice-annual dental cleanings. Interestingly, some families take their young children and introduce them to their dentist to start dental work from an incredibly early age. Sadly, the need for a family counselor is not treated with the same importance as the need for a family doctor whom we seek out for our physical health.

How different would it be for many families if a visit to the family counselor was given the same priority as the visit to the family doctor or dentist? Quite possibly, many family issues, conflicts, and even divorce might be averted or successfully resolved.

Many child suicide victims, gang members, or drug abusers could be detected early and corrective measures put in place.

11

Savings & Spending Strategies for Pre- and Post-Marital Counseling

---

Scripture teaches that "*there is a way that seems right unto a man, but the end thereof are the ways of death*" (Prov. 14:12 KJV). It is so easy for marriages and families to be torn apart by poor and unwise financial management. Money **does** matter. It represents more than just a medium of exchange. According to Grunlan (2013), money represents "power, love, status, and many other things such as security, confirmation of one's worth, and opportunities for self and family" (156).

In the New Testament, Jesus speaks more about money than heaven and hell combined. The basic concern of the Bible seems to be with man's attitude towards money. While we are counseled and cautioned not to love money because "*the love of money is the root of all evil*" (1 Tim. 6:10 KJV), it is wise to understand how to use it, whether you have little or much. Finance is a major cause of strife in a marriage. That is why two people contemplating marriage and becoming a couple need to explore this topic of money in depth (Grunlan 1984).

Here is a successful money management formula that any family can use to achieve balance, mutual respect, and a respectable financially secure future for your family. This approach can only work if the husband and wife are willing to combine their salaries and decide to work together as partners. This calls for love, trust, respect, and teamwork all wrapped in a package of open communication. This is a model for success for any couple regardless of income. It is God's desire for His people to be the head and not the tail.

> **In the New Testament, Jesus speaks more about money than heaven and hell combined. The basic concern of the Bible seems to be with man's attitude towards money.**

A marriage is like a business in which the husband and wife are partners. For a marriage and partnership to be successful, goals must be set, and an annual audit or stock-taking is made each year or as needed. The annual audit is important to ensure the family is on track to achieve their goals or reveal that they need to change something. Follow these eight steps and enjoy the blessings of the Lord.

1. **Appoint a business manager**. Decide who will be responsible for paying the bills when they become due and keep the partnership in equilibrium.

2. **Make a budget**. Grunlan (2013) suggests at least four purposes or values of budgeting for couples. He points out that a budget (1) maximizes income, (2) provides a realistic view of financial status, (3) opens communication, and (4) reduces tension. It allows a couple to invest in those things they value most. That is one of the reasons for prioritizing (159).

3. **Open three separate accounts under the following headings**:
   a. family's savings account;
   b. family's expense checking account; and
   c. family's personal spending account.

A. The Family's Savings Account

In this account, the family places all the family's savings (excluding mutual funds, IRA, annuity, etc.). This account includes a down payment for your first house, life-threatening emergency spending, a down payment to purchase a new car, and a college education. A pledge should be made between the couple that these funds should be used under no circumstances other than what is designated. Using any of these funds, even for the designated items, should be with mutual understanding. It is the family's savings account; therefore, no one person owns it or has exclusive claims to it.

An Eye-Opening Family Scenario:

Jim and Mary have been married for four years and have a two-year-old son named Timmy. They have established their three accounts for success and budgeted to save twenty thousand dollars ($20,000) in five years. The purpose of this five-year savings plan is to be able to make a down payment towards the purchase of their first home. They presently have eighteen thousand five hundred dollars ($18,500) saved towards this goal and have begun to look around for a community of choice, since they would reach their savings target in a few months.

One eventful day, Jim received a call from his brother Joe who told him that he needed five thousand dollars ($5,000) in two days; otherwise, he would be going to prison. He explained that this was a life-and-death situation, and Jim was his last resort. After Joe's sycophantic begging and pleading, Jim told him that he would have to go home and speak with his wife and get back to him that night. What if Mary were to refuse and hold out that their savings were only going to be used as designated? Jim would be faced with a dilemma by having to go back to his brother and say no—he cannot help.

This, in turn, would trigger the problem of ill feelings between Joe and Mary, which would be no fault of Mary. Jim had already given his brother Joe the impression that the money was available, but he had to speak with Mary first. This approach by Jim inadvertently would create a family rift and possible bitterness and resentment that could take years to heal or overcome. What might have been a better approach? Could there be a better response to Joe's request that would lead to a better outcome, regardless? Absolutely! Pay close attention and read inductively.

This is the correct response and the winning approach to the same scenario:

Jim listened to Joe's begging and pleading with interest mingled with measured scolding and counsel. He told Joe that he did not have any money, and he was sure that his wife, Mary, did not have any either. Certainly, he did not lie to his brother because the money saved did not belong to him or his wife —it was the family's money. At home, Jim related the story and the request from his brother to Mary.

Mary listened sympathetically and felt very sorry for Joe. Mary then turned to Jim and stated emphatically, "Jim, we cannot allow Joe to go to prison; he has been a good brother to you and uncle to our son." Jim interrupted, "Agreed, but how are we going to help when we have no money?" Mary suggested they push back their house purchase to the following year or make a smaller down payment and take the money from their family's savings. This was a huge sacrifice, but they were both in agreement that they would use the money from their family's savings to help Joe. They have just crossed a major hurdle through mutual understanding gained through respect, trust, and proper communication.

Later that evening, Jim called Joe and told him that he had informed Mary of the situation after arriving home. He told Joe that Mary was determined that they should find the money and help because he was a good brother and uncle to little Timmy. Jim told Joe that the money was coming from the down payment for their home, and he had Mary to thank for it. Joe was overjoyed and expressed his deep appreciation to Jim and was ready to drive over to thank Mary himself. What has this approach wrought? Firstly, it galvanized the family relationship between the brothers. Secondly, it provided a greater possibility of repayment because Joe did not perceive it so much as coming from his brother Jim, but instead from Jim's wife, Mary. Thirdly, it created a deeper bond with Mary and heightened respect for her. Lastly, if Joe were a jerk and a scammer and had no intention of paying back the money, this couple would have had every reason to refuse help to him should a future need arise, and he would prove himself to be unconscionable if he were to approach them again.

B. The Family's Expense Account

This second account must be a checking account and is used expressly for the payment of the family bills. It serves as an operating expense account and is managed and executed according to the budget. This is the account where the couple's salaries are deposited, and from which all other accounts are serviced and maintained by the business manager. While both names are on this account, only the family business manager uses it. The other party must know what to do if the business manager, for any reason, becomes incapacitated or is not available to service the account.

There should be planned time for the family to discuss the family's expense account. Some families may choose to do this quarterly, half-yearly, or annually. This account is the heartbeat of the family liquidity. It is like a bucket that draws water from a well. It must always have a cord that is long enough to reach the bottom of the well should the water level fall. The business manager must manage so that the expense account is never in the negative. The couple may choose to include the children in this family financial discussion and stock-taking. It is a learning session for children.

Getting the children involved has some positive outcomes. The children will know exactly how much spending money the family has, and they will know exactly how much money is put away for savings and why. Neither are they likely to make unreasonable financial demands on their parents when included in the financial picture.

C. The Family's Spending Account

The family budget must show how much the couple needs to spend as individuals. This expenditure should include but not be limited to travel, lunch, and possibly an allowance for miscellaneous spending. Please bear in mind that the couple, at this point, must view themselves as a team working to achieve a specific goal and to please their creator God in all that they do. Scripture teaches that the two have become one, therefore, they must work together (Mark 10:8–9). At the end of each year, the couple may choose to roll over their account balances into the family's savings account. God expects families to work together in an honest and dignified way, and this can only be accomplished when there is respect for the divine authority identified in Scripture.

According to Jay Adams (1973), the need exists for divine authority in counseling, and only biblical counseling possesses such authority. The **Basement Theory** is based on Scripture and follows the example of Jesus Christ, whose encounters were so life-changing that return visits were commonplace from those who wanted more of what He offered. The story of the Samaritan woman in John 4:4–26 provides the best example of one such counseling encounter with Jesus. Zacchaeus and the woman at the well are other stories where Jesus had just one counseling encounter. One meeting with Jesus was all it took for the work of transformation to take place. This is the essence of *Brief Therapy* with a solution-focused emphasis.

Mankind has always been in search of something outside of himself. Yet mankind fails to realize that he need not look beyond himself to find what he needs the most. What he needs has always been within his grasp. What mankind needs is peace with God. Peace with God establishes the vertical relationship that ultimately manifests itself in the horizontal relationship with his fellowmen. This is where true peace lies. If he has peace, many of his problems will vanish. The Lord Jesus Christ is the answer to this need, and only the individual who is connected both vertically and horizontally, the Christian, can proclaim the supply of this need. This is the supreme advantage that the Christian counselor has over all other counselors. The Scripture teaches that *"great peace have they which love thy law: and nothing shall offend them"* (Psa. 119:165 KJV), and, *"Blessed are the peacemakers: for they shall be called the children of God"* (Matt. 5:9 KJV).

The **Basement Theory** aims to meet with couples experiencing marital conflict and diagnose the source or root cause. After a diagnosis is made, spiritual counseling is provided that is *solution-focused* and specific to the diagnosed problems. The BTCCR technique will invariably reveal that the conflict is triggered by an unfulfilled need—or priorities not aligned with the partners. According to Crabb (1977), "Because humans are both physical beings and personal beings, they have both physical and personal needs" (79-80).

These unmet needs are generally the source or triggers for conflict. The pastoral counselor is responsible for understanding and knowing how to interpret the **Basement Theory** to unmask and reveal the problem(s) before leading the couple toward a solution. Two hours per session is generally recommended to spend with a couple from diagnosis to counseling intervention and homework. The nature of the diagnosed issues and resulting conflicts may require follow-up sessions using brief therapeutic interventions.

It is interesting to note that **Cross' Basement Theory for Couples' Conflict Resolution** is only a diagnostic tool. It is, therefore, the responsibility of the pastor to be educated and trained to use the recommended counseling interventions to guide the couple in resolving the conflict. This requires other areas of pastoral development that will not be covered in this book. Such areas include but are not limited to listening skills, understanding personalities, the sociology of the family, and cross-cultural or intercultural perspectives. It is very important to know the cause of a conflict, but it is more important to have the skill set to administer corrective treatment.

Resolution of the conflict and restoration of a broken relationship is dependent on both the couple's desire for wholeness and their application of the solutions presented by the counselor. Consequently, homework assignments will be necessary for most couples. Although the assignment does not necessitate the return of the couple to see the pastoral counselor, it is highly recommended that they return to ensure that the assignment is done correctly. This visit should be scheduled by the pastoral counselor before the couple leaves the office. After the second visit, which includes the sharing of homework assignments, all subsequent visits become the couple's sole prerogative.

Since the couple is not expected to return, no follow-up visits are scheduled for them. However, they will continue their work at home after being provided with the tools to continue the path to relationship and marital wholeness. One of the purposes of the homework is for counselees to develop problem-resolution and coping skills on their own. This is the primary reason why *Solution-Focused Brief Therapy* is one of the counseling intervention models chosen for the ***Basement Theory.*** It helps the couple not to depend on the pastoral counselor as their source of help. It is recommended that the pastoral counselor concludes the session with both parties holding hands and praying for each other. According to Adams (1973), the Christian minister and counselor must be willing to assume the full task of ministering to men and women who suffer from the pain and misery that stem from personal sin.

The pastoral counselor should be careful not to create a situation in which the counselees feel dependent on them. Homework helps them to work through issues and conflicts through love, forgiveness, and reconciliation. Homework helps them to develop the ability to do things together. It is almost impossible for any marriage to survive without the couple doing some things together.

Every married couple will need to understand the concept and value of love in confession, forgiveness, and reconciliation. Solution-focused, as opposed to problem-focused, is the biblical approach to marital conflict. Two people cannot live together without having some areas of disagreement and misunderstanding. According to Grunlan (2013), "There are five categories of differences between couples. These categories are taste, habits, values, thinking, and temperament. Differences generally do not destroy a marriage. It is how these differences are handled that determines the outcome of the marriage" (182-185). After the diagnosis is made and the root cause of the conflict is identified, it is time for the counselor to listen to the couple as they take their time to tell their stories. The good pastoral counselor will listen carefully as the burdened ones tell their stories. Careful notes must be taken, and interruptions should be made only to seek clarification. Telling their stories is not merely for sharing information but is also therapeutic in nature. Sometimes, one or both parties may become tearful. It is always a good thing for the counselor to show empathy by recognizing the intensity of the pain and hurt at this time and then pausing to offer specific prayers for the couple.

The Christian counselor must seek wisdom and guidance from the Holy Spirit through the medium of prayer to point out difficulty and show how it may be solved. The Christian must be aware of counseling needs beyond his or her skill set. While all problems have their root in sin, psychological problems requiring medical attention are beyond the skill set of the pastoral or Christian counselor. It is believed and accepted that most sicknesses are a result of the mind. It is, therefore, imperative that pastoral counselors know their limitations and be prepared to make the necessary referral.

12

Homework for the Couple

The following homework assignments are designed to help the couple grow in love, appreciation, and acceptance of each other as children of God. This is possible only through daily communion with God and communication with each other while working together.

1. **GOD'S EXPECTATION FOR MAN:** In Genesis 2:18 (KJV), God spoke clearly and said, *"It is not good that man should be alone."*

    a. List four things you believe God means when He said *"not good"* in Genesis 2:18. Example: The creation was not complete, so it was not good.

    _____

    _____

    _____

    _____

    b. Who initiates the marriage ceremony according to Genesis 2:22(b)?
        • Who was the father of the bride?

    _____

- Who blessed the wedding?

_____

- Who were the witnesses?

_____

c. List three implications this should have on your wedding and marriage.

_____

_____

_____

d. Marriage is referred to as a covenant in Malachi 2:14.
    - What is the meaning of the word "*covenant*"?

_____

_____

_____

    - What implication does it have for your marriage?

_____

_____

_____

e. Marriage is God's idea and plan for man. Therefore:
    - God can fix anything in the marriage that goes wrong (True or False).
    - Marriage is not a covenant—it is a contract (True or False).

- Under no circumstance should a Christian seek a divorce (True or False).

2. **PURPOSE DETERMINED BY GOD**

   a. Companionship
      - Why do you think Genesis 2:19–20 comes between Genesis 2:18 and 21–22?

      _____

      _____

      _____

      _____

      - Using the words "*alone*" and "*helpmeet*" in Genesis 2:18, what four conclusions can you draw that reflect God's purpose of companionship in marriage?

      _____

      _____

      _____

      _____

   b. Sexual intimacy in marriage.
      - What is your understanding of Genesis 2:24–25?

      _____

      _____

      _____

      _____

      _____

• Read 1 Corinthians 7:1–5 (the use of different translations is recommended). What conclusions have you drawn about the frequency of sexual relations?

_____

_____

_____

_____

_____

_____

• If biblical love is shared, what should be our focus in terms of sexual behavior?

_____

_____

_____

_____

_____

• Why is sex not just for procreation? Give four reasons.

_____

_____

_____

_____

_____

_____

c. Children (Gen. 1:27–28).
   • Considering these verses, do you think
     every couple should have children? (Yes
     or No) Explain.

   _____

   _____

   _____

   _____

   _____

   _____

   • Do you think marriage has to produce
     children to be considered a family? (Yes
     or No) Explain.

   _____

   _____

   _____

   _____

   _____

   • Do you think that a childless marriage is a
     reason for divorce? (Yes or No) Explain.

   _____

   _____

   _____

   _____

   _____

• Given Ephesians 5:22–32, what is one reason that God desires permanency in marriage?

_____

_____

_____

_____

_____

_____

3. **GOD DESIGNED MARRIAGE TO BE PERMANENT**
   (Matt. 19:3–19; 1 Cor. 7:10–16; Rom. 7:1–3; Mark 10:1–12; Luke 16:18)
   a. What is God's pleasure regarding marriage?

   _____

   _____

   _____

   b. Does God permit divorce? For what reason?

   _____

   _____

   _____

   c. If divorce occurs, is forgiveness still required of the offended party? (Yes or No) Explain.

   _____

   _____

   _____

4. **FUNCTIONS WITHIN MARRIAGE**

    a. Husband (Eph. 5:16–6:20; 1 Peter 3:7–9). What is your understanding of these commands?

        _____

        _____

        _____

        _____

    b. Given modernity, culture, and current laws, are these commands outdated? (Yes or No) Why?

        _____

        _____

        _____

        _____

        _____

    c. With privilege comes responsibility. List three responsibilities that come with headship.

        _____

        _____

        _____

        _____

        _____

d. Since the husband is to follow the example
   of Christ over His church, read John 13 and
   describe how Jesus exercised leadership.

   _____

   _____

   _____

   _____

   _____

   _____

   _____

e. List five ways you can lead your spouse
   after Christ's example.

   _____

   _____

   _____

   _____

   _____

   _____

   _____

   _____

   _____

13

Couples Conflict Resolution Question- naire: Towards Reconciliation

A conflict resolution questionnaire for married couples only (1 Pet. 3:1, 7-12).

Please answer all questions completely and as truthfully as far as you can remember.

Name_____

Date_____

No. of children_____   Age_____

Years of Marriage_____.   Tel. _____

True love is an unconditional commitment
to an imperfect person.   T or F

Love grows and anything that grows
requires time.   T or F

Anything that grows can die if it is not
nurtured and fed.   T or F

True love comes from God.   T or F

There can be true love without commitment. T or F

The things to which you are committed
help shape who you are.   T or F

The things to which you are committed
can help build you or destroy you.   T or F

For a marriage to succeed, all it needs is love. T or F

Commitment is more important than love
in a marriage.   T or F

We ultimately become whatever we are
committed to.   T or F

Wealth and fame are the enemies of every
marriage.   T or F

It is okay to cheat on your spouse if it
enhances your business.   T or F

It is okay to cheat on your spouse if he or
she will never find out.   T or F

Cheating can be habit-forming and addictive. T or F

Speaking the truth only makes the
wrongdoer look good.   T or F

Speaking the whole truth is the first step
in rebuilding trust.   T or F

It is always a sign of sincerity when the
guilty party confesses after being caught.   T or F

In a marriage, it is always better to make
sleeping dogs lie than to bring up past
infidelity of which your spouse was unaware. T or F

Protection of the guilty third person
is always a sign of poor judgment and
questionable sincerity.   T or F

Contact with the third party after
unfaithfulness has occurred is a sign of
maturity and should not be questioned by
the faithful spouse.   T or F

Once forgiveness is given, the guilty party
should be treated as if no wrong was ever
done.   T or F

Unfaithfulness in a marriage is a mark of
disrespect but not selfishness.   T or F

To change your life, you must change the
way you think and sometimes the friends
you keep.   T or F

There is a thought behind everything we do. T or F

People who say they will stop doing sinful
acts and change are lying to themselves

and will repeat the same sin later in life.
Only God can help to change their sinful
behavior.   T or F

Please read 2 Corinthians 5:17–20 and 1 John 1:9
and continue.

True repentance is Godly sorrow for sin
and not sorrow you were caught.   T or F

Once a person is caught, they will forsake
the sinful act and live right.   T or F

There can be no forgiveness without
genuine confession.   T or F

True reconciliation always comes after
confession.   T or F

Genuine forgiveness, repentance, and
reconciliation are all divine attributes. T or F

Additional Resources to Use with Cross' Basement Theory

1. Baucom, Donald H. and Norman Epstein. 2013. *Cognitive-Behavioral Marital Therapy.* Routledge.
2. Worthington, Everett L. 1989. *Marriage Counseling: A Christian Approach to Counseling Couples.* IVP Academic.
3. Boyd-Franklin, Nancy. 2006. *Black Families in Therapy: Understanding the African American Experience.* Guilford Press.
4. Wright, H. Norman. 1989. *Marital Counseling: A Biblical, Behavioral, Cognitive Approach.*
5. Swihart, Judson J. and Gerald C. Richardson. 1987. *Counseling in Times of Crisis.* W Publishing Group.
6. Jacobson, Neil S. 1996. *Acceptance and Change in Couple Therapy: A Therapist's Guide to Transforming Relationships.*
7. Sanders, Randolph K. 1997. *Christian Counseling Ethics: A Handbook for Therapists, Pastors & Counselors.* InterVarsity Press.

Three Basement Theory Vignettes

These three vignettes will highlight the effectiveness of **Cross' Basement Theory** as a conflict resolution diagnostic technique. The first vignette identifies a couple's first session in pre-marital counseling. The other two vignettes identify couples who are married and are experiencing conflict in their marriages. Each vignette was used with permission; however, the real names have been changed to protect the identities of the individuals.

VIGNETTE # 1

Tony and Ann met and fell in love. They are both Christians from the same faith background but attend church in various locations. Tony and Ann are both professionals and are successful in their jobs. They sought pre-marital counsel from us and subsequently set their wedding date twelve months in the future. As always, and for any couple in counseling, they were introduced to the **Basement Theory,** which serves as part of the general intake information on couples.

The interpretation of the *Conflict Resolution* technique revealed the following: Tony placed sex at the very bottom of his sixteen-item list of priorities, while Ann placed sex at number four on her sixteen-item list of priorities. Tony placed children at number four on his sixteen-item list, and Ann placed children at number five on hers. As we went down the list in interpretation and explanation, when we got to sex at number four for Ann, she discovered that Tony had sex at number sixteen. She screamed at him in utter surprise, the following, "Jesus Christ, Tony! Are you impotent?"

Tony was given the opportunity to respond after the shock of Ann's body language and surprising question sunk in. With a smile, Tony responded by saying that he placed sex at the bottom of his list of priorities because sex was not a priority for him now since he was not married, but if he were to redo the assessment after they were married, he would probably have it at four or five. Ann interrupted and stated that she was very much relieved, but at first, she was very confused because she could not understand how Tony had children at number four and sex at the very last. Again, Tony clarified that since he had two sons from his first marriage, taking care of them was a priority for him. They were both commended for keeping themselves sexually pure, as the BTCCR tool revealed through their communication.

The interjection of children as a priority for Tony revealed to us the need to ask the right questions to uncover Ann's feelings and support for Tony's children. It was also revealed that Ann wanted to have children of her own and did not plan to waste any time starting their own family together. Therefore, children were placed at number five on her list of priorities. Ann explained that she was already in her late thirties and had no intention of waiting until she was forty to have her first child. They were counseled to spend the next six months bonding and regularly doing things together before pregnancy.

Early pregnancy in a marriage can create a conflict for the couple because sometimes the wife makes the mistake of giving all her attention to the unborn child in the womb and neglecting her husband. Sometimes early pregnancy sickness is an unanticipated factor for the couple, and they may not have the financial capacity to address it. For this reason, among others, an earlier-than-expected pregnancy can potentially drive a wedge between couples.

The **Basement Theory** helped us to provide specific counsel relating to potential conflict in Tony and Ann's marriage. They later signed the mandatory return for their post-marital counseling, which is due to take place six months after their wedding. They both expressed their profound appreciation for the counsel and promised to keep their post-marital counseling date six months after they get married.

VIGNETTE # 2

John and Mary have been married for fourteen years. Mary is now retired but John continues to work as a chaplain and itinerant pastor. They both heard about the *Basement Theory* and wished to get permission to use it in their ministry. We told them that they were welcome to do so on condition that they applied it to themselves first. They both agreed to use the technique right there in the living room of our home. We sat closer as we began to provide the interpretation. Everything on the sixteen-item priority list for John and Mary looked very good, except the topic of education.

Again, we explained the process and method of interpretation. John had education at number four on his list of priorities while Mary had education at number ten on her list. We commended them both for completing the instrument with only one area of conflict or potential conflict. When the area of conflict or potential conflict was disclosed, John was asked to explain why education appeared to be an area of conflict in their marriage. John opted for

Mary to answer the question. Mary, at this point, sat up in her seat and turned the question back to John, who insisted that Mary should be the one to answer. We turned to Mary for the second time while hinting that somebody needed to answer.

At this stage, Mary jumped to her feet, much to the surprise of my wife and myself, and shouted with an annoying voice, "Well, Reverend Cross and Mrs. Cross, let me tell you straight—this man has just completed his master's in counseling and wants to go and do his doctorate? Not over my dead body!" We asked, "Why would you not want him to do his doctorate?" Still standing, pointing straight at her husband, and appearing to be visibly upset, she responded, "Reverend Cross, Mrs. Cross, I supported my husband in achieving all his education goals. I am now retired, and all I have is a high school diploma. Doctorate? Not over my dead body!" Mary sat back quietly, breathing heavily while looking away from John.

It was obvious that this subject had been a talking point in their home and had now grown into an area of conflict. Mary appeared to be upset and hurt, and now their marriage needed counseling intervention. Fortunately, they were willing to be counseled and get whatever help they could. *Solution-Focused Brief Therapy* and *Cognitive Behavioral Therapy* were the interventions of choice. Their spiritual foundation and love for each other also helped.

For the first time, Mary appeared to have had the opportunity to express exactly how she was feeling in the presence of someone apart from John. Mary shared with us that she felt that she was heard for the first time because she was able to express herself without being interrupted. She also expressed that she was feeling a sense of inferiority. John interrupted and gave the rationale for his reason for wanting to forge ahead academically. He saw himself as the head of the family and chief provider. Therefore, it was his responsibility to ensure that he was educated so he could provide for his family.

Fortunately, when we helped John recognize that he was leaving his wife too far behind in the field of academia, he was understanding, compromising, and supportive. We explained to John that Mary was now experiencing an inferiority complex, and this could affect her self-esteem and attitude towards him. John loves his wife and did not intend to hurt her deliberately; nevertheless, she was hurting silently.

Outside of the *Basement Theory*, such a conflict could have gone undiagnosed, and another potentially good marriage could have become another statistic. John agreed to wait until Mary completed her first degree before continuing his doctoral studies. Mary was happy with the adjustment and compromise. Can you think of any couple, even in your church, that could be going through a similar situation today?

VIGNETTE # 3

Mr. and Mrs. Jones have been married for twenty-eight years. They have a twenty-six-year-old daughter who still lives in the home with them. The couple lives in Orlando, Florida, but Mr. Jones's work takes him to Texas regularly. Mrs. Jones called seeking marriage counseling but was concerned that her husband would not come. After much begging and pleading, the husband finally decided to accompany her for their first session before he journeyed back to Texas. They were introduced to the **Basement Theory** and set out to apply the diagnostic tool.

On completion of the information required by the BTCCR, they came together for the interpretation. Mr. and Mrs. Jones attended church occasionally but were not committed Christians. The diagnostic interpretation revealed that they were having conflicts in the areas of friendship and sex. Mr. Jones placed friendship at number twelve on his list of priorities, and Mrs. Jones placed friendship at number six. Mr. Jones also placed sex at number nine, while Mrs. Jones had sex at number five. They were commended for having only two conflict areas after being married for twenty-eight years.

When the two areas of conflict were finally revealed, Mr. Jones became visibly uncomfortable. When he was asked if he was okay, he said he was okay but just shocked. We inquired why he was shocked about the diagnosis and he responded that it was spot on. Up to this point, Mrs. Jones kept quiet but was speaking volumes with her body language. Mrs. Jones was asked what she had to say about the revelation of friendship and sex as areas of conflict or potential conflict in her marriage. She responded and said that her husband would be glad to address those areas and agreed that those were areas of conflict in their twenty-eight-year-old marriage.

We turned to Mr. Jones to explain the revelation by asking him a direct question as to why there was a conflict in his marriage with friendship and sex. Mr. Jones turned to his wife and asked her if she was sure she wanted him to respond. She told him to go right ahead and respond. So, he began his response this way: "Dr. and Mrs. Cross, I am glad I came. I did not want to come because we have gone through several counseling sessions with different counselors, all to no avail. I told my wife that I have come to the end of the road because I just cannot live like this anymore. That was when she reached out to you.

This was going to be my last try. We have been married for twenty-eight years—*twenty-eight years!* And I still feel like my wife does not love me."

We asked, "Why do you feel that she does not love you?" He answered, "Dr. Cross, ever since we got married, my wife has been putting her friends before me and even our marriage." We asked, "Can you share one instance in which she puts her friends before you?" He replied, "Sir, I spend a lot of time on the road, driving from here to Texas. When I come home, she has no time for me, always visiting with her friends, and when she is not visiting, she is always on the phone. When I complained she told me that when I am not there, these are the people that keep her company. Dr. Cross, our daughter lives in the home with us and she even complains about her mother's obsession with these friends. Now I have gotten to the point where I have even lost my sex drive."

We said, "Mrs. Jones, those are serious complaints. What do you have to say about your husband's complaints, and how does it make you feel?" She responded, "Well, Dr. Cross, we have been struggling with this for a long time, but I do not see what I am doing that is so wrong. I love my husband, and I never keep myself away from him; he just started to drift away. I know it is very serious, and when one of my friends told me about you, I did not hesitate to call because I don't want my husband to leave me." At this point, tears welled in her eyes and cascaded down her cheeks.

Counsel specific to the needs of this couple was provided to open the eyes of Mrs. Jones so she could understand that her husband should be her best friend and all other friends should be put on hold when he is around, especially if they are not his friends. At the end of the session, Mr. Jones inquired as to how soon, before he left for Texas, he could return for a follow-up visit.

CONCLUSION

I encourage the use of the *Cross' Basement Theory for Couples Conflict Resolution* (BTCCR) by all pastors. If used correctly, it can make a huge difference in every Christian congregation. It is the responsibility of the pastor—the shepherd of the flock—to utilize this tool and help couples in conflict. The hourglass of time for this world seems to have already run out; we are therefore living on borrowed time.

People are different and differences invariably can create conflict in any relationship—marriages between Christians are no exception. Conflict seems to be one of the devil's main tools used to bring about dissension among God's people. Calvary was the center of conflict where the forces of good and evil collided head-on—the force of love and the force of hate. The power of love represented by Christ won over the love of power represented by Satan.

At Calvary, Jesus gained an eternal victory over the conflict of good and evil. Every Christian pastor needs to understand that we are living in a world of conflict. Alan Redpath was once quoted as saying, "If you are a Christian pastor, you are always in a crisis, either in the middle of one, coming out of one, or going into one." Pastors must understand that the whole purpose of the incarnation is the fact that Christ must die. He could not die as God, so His divinity had to be cloaked in humanity so he could die as a man. Like Methuselah, Christ was born to die, creating a conflict.

The devil, who is the enemy of all families, especially targets Christian families. Christian churches all over the world are experiencing internal conflicts. There is conflict caused by creeping compromises, conflict from distorted views of the truth, and conflict caused by man's basic sinful nature. Conflicts are being compounded because many people cannot determine which issues are critical to their faith and which are merely self-aggrandizement and a matter of personal interpretation. *Cross' Basement Theory for Couples Conflict Resolution* (BTCCR) applies primarily to couples in a conflict that may include interpersonal relationship conflict.

However, it is interesting to note that family conflicts inadvertently affect the church. Self-preservation and the desire to win are all reasons for conflict in a relationship. In the church and groups, the general struggle for power, position, and prestige are some of the causes. Often, the real issue gets lost. Global signs and dissension are forecasting that this is not a world that is about to experience utopia. The end of this present world as we know it is fast approaching. Scripture teaches that when a man thinks that it is peace and safety, sudden destruction will come (1 Thess. 5:1–4). In the meantime, we must be busy restoring broken relationships to fulfill the ministry of reconciliation for which we have been charged as believers. It behooves us, therefore, to treat each other as family and understand that life is all about relationships.

References

Adams, Jay, Edward 1979. *A Theology of Christian Counseling: More than Redemption.* Zondervan.

Adams, Jay Edward. 1973. *The Christian Counselor's Manual: The Sequel and Companion Volume to Competent to Counsel.* Baker Publishing Group (MI).

Clinton, Timothy E., Archibald D. Hart, and George W. Ohlschlager. 2005. *Caring for People God's Way: Personal and Emotional Issues, Addictions, Grief, and Trauma.* Thomas Nelson Inc.

Clinton, Tim, and John Trent. 2009. *The Quick-Reference Guide to Marriage & Family Counseling.* Baker Books.

Crabb, Larry. 1977. *Effective Biblical Counseling: A Model for Helping Caring Christians Become Capable Counselors.* Zondervan.

Gorer, Geoffrey. 1965. *Death, Grief, and Mourning.* New York: Doubleday.

Grunlan, Stephen A. 1984. *Marriage and the Family: A Christian Perspective.* Zondervan.

Grunlan, Stephen. 2013. *Marriage and the Family: A Christian Perspective.* Wipf and Stock Publishers.

Moyers, Bill D., and Betty S. Flowers. 1993. *Healing and the Mind.* New York: Doubleday.

Richardson, Ronald W. 2010. *Couples in Conflict: A Family Systems Approach to Marriage Counseling.* Fortress Press.

Sperry, Len. 2012. *Spirituality in Clinical Practice: Theory and Practice of Spiritually-Oriented Psychotherapy.* Routledge.

Walsh, Froma. 2009. *Spiritual Resources on Family Therapy.* Guilford Press.

Worthington, Everett L. 1999. *Hope-Focused Marriage Counseling: A Guide to Brief Therapy.* InterVarsity Press.